THE KITCHEN

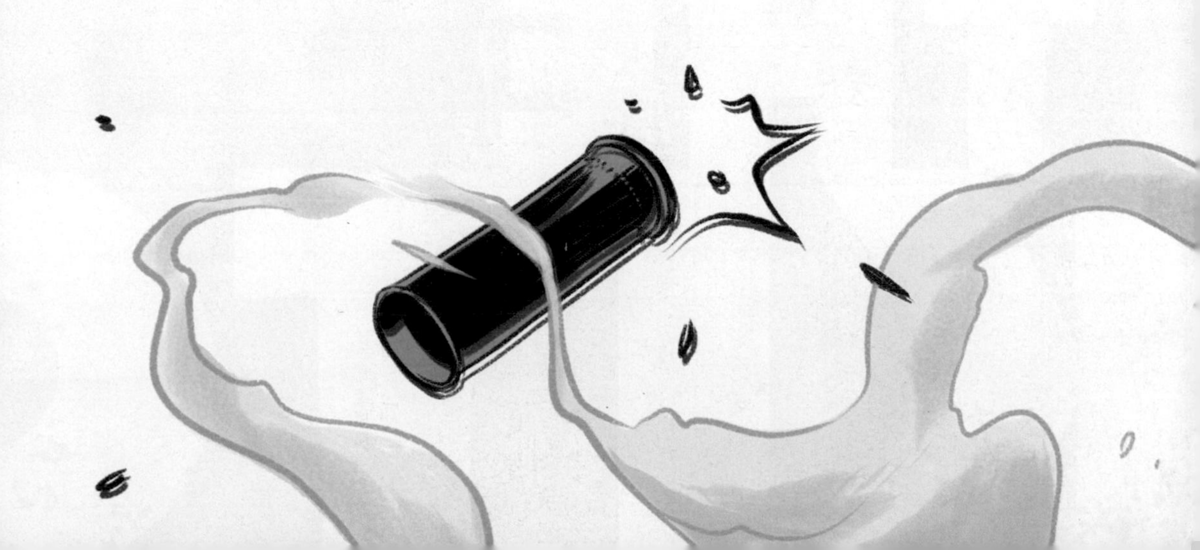

THE
KITC

OLLIE MASTERS Writer
MING DOYLE Artist
JORDIE BELLAIRE Colorist
CLEM ROBINS Letterer
BECKY CLOONAN Cover Art and Original Series Covers
THE KITCHEN created by **OLLIE MASTERS** and **MING DOYLE**

HEN

THE KITCHEN

DC Comics
2900 West Alameda Avenue
Burbank, CA 91505
Printed in the USA. First Printing.
ISBN: 978-1-4012-5773-6.

Library of Congress Cataloging-in-Publication Data

Masters, Ollie.
The Kitchen / Ollie Masters, writer ; Ming Doyle, artist.
pages cm
ISBN 978-1-4012-5773-6 (paperback)
1. Gangs—Comic books, strips, etc. 2. Hell's Kitchen (New York, N.Y.)—Comic books, strips, etc. 3. Graphic novels. I. Doyle, Ming, illustrator. II. Title.
PN6727.M24645K58 2015
741.5'973—dc23

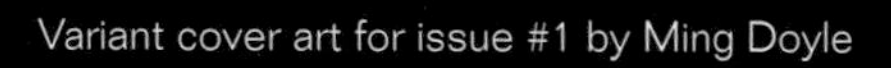

Variant cover art for issue #1 by Ming Doyle

HELL'S KITCHEN. THE SEVENTIES.
CASEY'S PUB
PUB
CHUK
YOU SHOULDA KEPT YOUR FUCKIN' MOUTH SHUT, FREDDIE.

PUB
PUB
PUB
PUB
POLICE

SOME PEOPLE YOU CAN'T HELP BUT NOTICE.
THEY IMPOSE THEMSELVES ON THE WORLD.
♪ WE HAD SAILED SEVEN YEARS WHEN THE MIZZENS BROKE OUT, AND OUR SHIP LOST HER WAY IN THE FOG.
AND THE WHALE OF A CREW WAS REDUCED DOWN TO TWO, 'TWAS MESELF AND THE CAPTAIN'S OLD DOG. ♪
...THE EVIDENCE CLEARLY SHOWS THAT THESE MEN...
JIMMY. A LOAN SHARK. A THIEF. A HOOD FROM THE KITCHEN.
HE IMPOSED HIMSELF ON THE WORLD.

WE FIND THE ACCUSED GUILTY ON ALL COUNTS...
...AND I SENTENCE YOU TO...
...AND THE POOR OLD DOG WAS DROWNED, I'M THE LAST OF THE IRISH ROVER.
C'MON, GUYS, LET'S GET IT FUCKIN' OVER WITH.
DON'T WORRY, OWEN. YOUR BEST CUSTOMERS'LL BE BACK IN FIVE YEARS. THREE WITH GOOD BEHAVIOR.
FAT FUCKIN' CHANCE AH' THAT!
AND WHEN HE WE TO PRISON...
...HE LEFT BIG SHOES TO FILL.

SHARPEN YOUR TEETH

JORDAN'S CONVENIE
SHORT AGAIN...

OWEN.
MRS. BRENNAN.
Budweiser

HOW'S EVERYTHING AT HOME, MRS. BRENNAN?
OKAY, I GUESS. THE BOYS ARE MISSIN' THEIR DAD, BUT YOU KNOW...
BOYS DO NEED THEIR PA.
WHAT ABOUT THE OTHER SIDE AH' THINGS? HOW'S JACK GETTIN' ON RUNNIN' THE CREW?
HE TRIES, BUT HE AIN'T GOT IT IN HIM TO BE LIKE JIMMY.
AYE, FEW DO.
HE'S A SOLDIER, NOT A LEADER.
AND HE'S LOSIN' RESPECT OUT THERE.
I WOULDN'T WORRY NONE.
BEFORE YOU KNOW IT, JIMMY'LL BE OUT AND THINGS'LL BE BACK TO NORMAL.
YEAH, WELL SOMETHIN'S GOTTA CHANGE AND SOON.
OTHER-WISE HE AIN'T GONNA HAVE ANYTHIN' LEFT TO COME BACK TO.

HEY, KATH...
RAVEN.
DRINK? I'VE GOT SOME WINE.
YEAH.
WHAT YOU MAKIN'?
SODA BREAD AND OTATO SOUP.
JESUS, THAT SAME IRISH SHIT MOM USED TO MAKE US WHEN WE WERE KIDS?
YEAH, WELL, WE CAN'T ALL AFFORD TO GO OUT TO DINNER EVERY NIGHT.

HOW YOU DOIN' FOR MONEY?
IT'S TOUGH. JOHNNY HAD SOME PUT AWAY BUT...YOU KNOW...
YEAH, I KNOW.
THE AMOUNT OF MONEY THAT PASSED THROUGH THEIR HANDS, YOU'D THINK THERE'D BE MORE UNDER THE MATTRESS.
AT LEAST YOU STILL GOT THE COLLECTION MONEY COMIN' IN.
WHAT D'YOU MEAN?
ALL THAT MONEY JOHNNY PUT OUT ON THE STREET.
DON'T TELL ME YOU HAVEN'T BEEN COLLECTIN' FOR HIM.
HE DIDN'T SAY ANYTHIN' ABOUT COLLECTIN' FOR HIM.
HE PROBABLY DIDN'T THINK HE'D HAVE TO!

SO YOU BEEN COLLECTIN' FOR JIMMY?
YEAH!
THIS AIN'T THE SAME AS BEFORE, RAVEN.
NORMALLY AT LEAST ONE OF THEM'D STILL BE ON THE STREET TO COLLECT FOR EVERY-ONE.
WITH THE THREE OF THEM INSIDE WE GOTTA DO IT FOR 'EM.
AIN'T JACK RUNNIN' THINGS NOW? WHY CAN'T HE DO IT?
HE'S FAMILY AND I LOVE HIM BUT HE AIN'T RUNNIN' SHIT. HE CAN BARELY COLLECT FOR HIM-SELF.
WHAT ABOUT ANGIE?
HAS SHE BEEN COLLECTIN' FOR ROB?
FUCK, IF YOU DON'T KNOW TO DO IT, SHE WON'T.
I'LL SPEAK TO HER AND WE'LL ALL GO OUT TOGETHER.
C'MON, WITH OUR HUSBANDS, WHO'S GONNA FUCK WITH US?

FOR FUCK'S SAKE, RAVEN, DON'T WAVE THAT AROUND.
WHAT IF A COP SEES YOU?
I WAS JUST COUNTIN' THIS. IT'S SHORT BY TWO HUNDRED.
SOME-TIMES IT'S SHORT.
SO PEOPLE ARE RIPPIN' US OFF AND YOU DON'T CARE?
AS LONG AS WE'RE GETTING MONEY IN, IT DON'T MATTER IF WE'RE SHORT BY A FEW HUNDRED.
WE'LL GET IT ALL IN THE END ANY-WAY.
SO WHAT WE GONNA DO IF THEY WON'T PAY US ANY-THIN'?

PIZZA
McKINNO
HEY, YOU FRANKY?
YEAH? WHAT YOU NEED?
RIGHT NOW I NEED YOU TO GIVE ME THE MONEY YOU OWE HER HUSBAND, ROB DILLON.
McKINNO
I GOT A BAD FEELING ABOUT THIS GUY...
WHAT? LOOK, LADY, I JUST FINISHED WORK AN' I WANNA GO HOME. I DON' NEED THIS SHIT RIGHT NOW.

YOU CAN GO HOME WHEN YOU GIVE ME THE MONEY YOU OWE HER HUSBAND--
HER IN THE CAR?
YEAH! HER IN THE FUCKIN' CAR!
LISTEN, LADY, ROB NEVER SAID NOTHIN' ABOUT NO WIFE. ANYWAY, I HEARD BRENNAN'S CREW GOT PUT AWAY.
YOU STILL OWE THEM THE FUCKIN' MONEY!
LADY, PLEASE JUST GET THE FUCK OUTTA HERE, OKAY? I AIN' GOT TIME FOR THIS.

YOU WOP FUCK! DO YOU KNOW WHO MY FUCKIN' HUSBAND IS--?
CRACK
DO I KNOW WHO YOUR HUSBAND IS? DO YOU KNOW WHO THE FUCK I AM?!
I COULD GIVE A FUCK WHO YOUR OLD MAN IS.
I AIN' GIVIN' SOME BITCH MY MONEY JUST 'CAUSE SHE SAYS SO.
SO GET OUTTA MY FACE!
KATH!
FOR FUCK'S SAKE!
WHEN KATH AND JIMMY FIRST GOT TOGETHER, HE TOOK HER TO CASEY'S ON A DATE...

WHAT THE HELL IS THIS? GET HER OUTTA HERE ALREADY.
C'MON, HONEY, LET'S GO HOME.
HE... HE CAN'T DO THAT TO ME.
FUCKIN' BITCH!
AND SOME GUY WHO DIDN'T KNOW JIMMY CRACKED A JOKE ABOUT HIS SHOES.
SO JIMMY STABBED HIM IN THE THROAT.
WHERE'D HE GO?
PLEASE, KATH, LET'S JUST GO BEFORE THINGS GET WORSE.
AFTERWARDS, SHE ASKED HIM HOW HE COULD DO SOMETHING LIKE THAT OVER A JOKE.

"KATH, WITH WHAT I DO, PEOPLE GOTTA SEE YOU AS SOMEONE NOT TO FUCK WITH.
"YOU GOTTA BE UNTOUCHABLE.
"SO IF SOMEONE DISRESPECTS YOU, EVEN IF IT'S JUST A FUCKIN' JOKE ABOUT YOUR SHOES, YOU FUCK 'EM UP SO BAD NO ONE'LL EVER CRACK WISE AGAIN.
"BECAUSE IF YOU LET SOMEONE CRACK WISE ABOUT YOU AND YOU DON'T DO NOTHIN' ABOUT IT? PEOPLE'LL THINK YOU'RE WEAK."

WHA', NO, PLEASE STO--

BLAM
AAAHHHH!

"AND WEAK PEOPLE... THEY DON'T SURVIVE IN THIS FOR LONG."
WHERE THE FUCK ARE YOU, FRANKY?
CHECK HIS POCKETS.
WE CAME HERE TO GET OUR MONEY.
WHAT?
WE NEED TO GET HIM TO A HOSPITAL.
OH, SHIT!
WE'VE SERIOUSLY FUCKED UP HERE.
WE FUCKIN' KNOW THAT! WE GOTTA--
NO, WE'VE SERIOUSLY FUCKED UP. HE'S FRANKY CASTELLANO. TONY CASTELLANO'S BROTHER!
RAVEN, YOUR FUCKIN' SISTER HERE JUST FUCKED UP THE BROTHER OF A MADE GUY.
WHAT ARE WE GONNA DO NOW?
THE FUCK...?

KATH KNEW SHE'D **FUCKED UP,** BUT SHE DIDN'T CARE.
BECAUSE RIGHT THEN, STANDING OVER **FRANKY CASTELLANO'S** BLEEDING BODY--
--KATH FELT **UNTOUCHABLE.**
SHALVEY MOTORS
NNON'S

A FEW DAYS AFTER THEY'D LEFT FRANKY BLEEDING IN THE STREET, THEY FOUND OUT HE WAS ALIVE IN THE HOSPITAL.
KATH HAD BEATEN HIM INTO A COMA SO DEEP THAT THE DOCTORS DIDN'T THINK HE'D EVER WAKE UP.
SO THEY FIGURED THEY WERE IN THE CLEAR AND GOT BACK TO WORK.
AFTER A FEW WEEKS EVERY-ONE IN THE KITCHEN KNEW THEY WERE RUNNING THINGS FOR THEIR HUSBANDS.
AND JIMMY'S NAME STILL CARRIED WEIGHT BETWEEN 34TH AND 59TH STREETS SO EVERYONE WENT ALONG WITH IT.
BUT EVEN THOUGH THEY NEVER SPOKE ABOUT IT, THE GIRLS COULDN'T HELP THINKING...

HOW LONG CAN YOU LIVE ON SOMEONE ELSE'S NAME?
JUS' GIVE US THE FUCKIN' MONEY. I'M SICKA' COMIN' DOWN HERE ASKIN' FOR IT.
I AIN'T GOT IT, MAN, I SWEAR. JUST GIMME A FEW MORE
AAAAAHHHH
WHAT'S GOIN' ON HERE?
WHAT THE FUCK'S IT GOTTA DO WITH YOU?

YOU WANT SUMA' THIS? FUCK OFF!
YOU SHOULD LEARN TO STAY OUTTA OTHER PEOPLE'S BUSINESS!
NOW YOU GONNA PAY BEFORE I DO SOME SERIOUS FUCKIN' DAMAGE TO THAT LEG?
HUUHHGG

I'M NOT GONNA BE A FUCKIN' PIMP.
IT'S JUST AN IDEA, RAVEN.
YEAH, WELL LAST TIME YOU HAD AN IDEA YOU PUT A GUY INNA' COMA, KATH.
ALL I'M SAYIN' IS WE'RE MAKIN' MONEY BUT WE COULD BE MAKIN' MORE AND IT'S A CLEAN BUSINESS--
CLEAN? HAVE YOU SEEN TIMES SQUARE LATELY?
IT'S CLEAN IF YOU DO IT RIGHT.
FUCK, EVEN DAD USED TO RUN GIRLS OUTTA HIS CLUB.
IF YOU'RE TRYIN' TO WIN ME OVER, YOU SHOULD LEAVE THAT PRICK OUT OF IT.
I KNOW YOU'VE FELT LIKE THE FUCKIN' DON OF HELL'S KITCHEN SINCE YOU FUCKED UP FRANKY, BUT YOU AIN'T DAD.
AND IF YOU'VE GOT ANY FUCKIN' SENSE, YOU DON'T WANT TO BE--
KLINK

SORRY, GIRLS. DON' MEAN TO INTERRUPT, BUT MY NAME'S NICKY LUBRETZI AN' I JUS' HEARD YOU TALKIN' ABOUT MY GOOD BUDDY FRANKY.
SUCH A SHAME WHAT HAPPENED TO HIM.
HEARD IT WAS A FEW GIRLS FROM THE KITCHEN WHO DID 'IM.
HOW DO YOU--
I WON' GET INTO THE NITTY GRITTY OF HOW, BUT I KNOW--
--YOU--
--BEAT THE SHIT OUTTA THE BROTHER OF A MADE GUY. AN' EVEN IF YER PROTECTED, YER NOT THAT PROTECTED.
SO HERE'S HOW IT'S GONNA BE. YOU GIVE ME--
--LET'S SAY... TWENNY LARGE. OR FRANKY'S BROTHER HEARS ALL ABOUT WHAT YOU DID.
I'LL BE BACK NEXT TUESDAY AFTER CLOSIN' TIME TO COLLECT THE MONEY. HAVE A GOOD DAY, LADIES.

YOU FUCKIN' BITCH! WHAT THE FUCK'VE YOU GOT US INTO?
IT'S FINE. WE'LL FIND THE MONEY.

THAT'S ALL I HAVE.
YOU OWE MY HUSBAND EIGHT FUCKIN' GRAND.
YEAH... BUT I PAY A HUNDRED A WEEK. I CAN'T PAY ALL THAT IN ONE GO.
IT'S MY MONEY AND I'M TELLIN' YOU I NEED IT ALL NOW.
SORRY, ANGIE, BUT IT JUST DON'T WORK LIKE THAT. YOUR HUSBAND AND ME, WE GOT A DEAL.
SUPPLIES
ASSHOLE.

DON' SHOOT!

HEY, GUYS!
WHAT'S THIS?
SIX HUNDRED BUCKS!
WHAT THE HELL? NOT EVEN A WELL DONE? WHAT'S GOIN' ON?
THEY LET TOMMY OUT.

HOW THE HELL DID THAT PSYCHO GET OUT?
THE DOCTORS AT THE NUTHOUSE SAY HE'S CURED.
LOOK, AIN'T THIS A GOOD THING? ALL THIS SHIT WE'RE IN WITH NICKY, HE CAN HELP US.

YOU THINK HE'S GONNA FUCKIN' HELP US?
IF WE'RE LUCKY AND HE DOESN'T KILL US FOR ALL THE SHIT WE CAUSED, YOU THINK HE'S GONNA LET US KEEP EARNIN'?
IS THAT SUCH A BAD THING? HE'S BEEN IN THIS SINCE THE BEGINNIN'. THIS WHOLE OPERATION'S BASICALLY HIS AN' JIMMY'S.
SHOULDN'T WE JUST GIVE IT BACK TO HIM AND GO BACK TO OUR LIVES?
THIS WAS JUST MEANT TO BE A TEMPORARY THING ANYWAY...RIGHT, KATH?

GET THE FUCK OUTTA HERE, GEORGE!

FUCK'S SAKE...
GEORGE? HONEY, I'M SORRY FOR SWEARIN'. THINGS ARE... THINGS ARE JUST TOUGH RIGHT NOW.
BUT IT'LL BE OKAY. I'M GOIN' TO FIX EVERYTHIN'.
NO ONE'S GONNA TAKE THIS FROM US.

LADIES, HOW THE FUCK AH' YA DOIN'?
WHAT? NO SMILES?
SO YOU GIRLS HAVE MY MONEY OR WHAT?
CASEY
UB

I'D SAY THIS IS ABOUT NINE GRAND LIGHT. AM I RIGHT?
THIS IS THE BEST WE COULD DO. WE AIN'T GANGSTERS--
I DUNNO, YOU LOOKED THE PART WHEN YOU BEAT THE SHIT OUTTA FRANKY.
AN' ELEVEN GRAND AIN'T BAD.
SO HOW ABOUT SOME DRINKS?
C'MON. YOU GIRLS NEED TO LIGHTEN UP.
SO YOU DON'T CARE THAT WE'RE SHORT?

C'MON, YOU'RE NOT THAT FUCKIN' STUPID.
LET ME GIVE YA' A LITTLE "GANGSTER" LESSON, SEEIN' AS YER SO KEEN TO LEARN.
YOU DON'T LEND SOMEONE MONEY TO GET IT BACK ON TIME. YOU DO IT FOR THE FUCKIN' INTEREST.
SO I'M GONNA TAKE THIS MONEY, BUT YOU GOTTA PAY ON THE NINE GRAND.
AND THE JUICE ON THAT IS FIFTEEN PERCENT A WEEK.
WHAT?!
FACE IT GIRLS, YOU FUCKED UP BAD...

EVERYONE EXPECTED IT TO BE KATH.
AND WHAT'S GOING TO STOP US PUTTIN' YOU IN A FUCKIN' COMA SAME AS FRANKY?
THAT'S A GOOD POINT. BUT SEE, I CAME PREPARED.
GIMME YOUR FUCKIN' GUN, KATH.
BUT ANGIE HAD SEEN SOMETHING WHEN KATH FUCKED UP FRANKY CASTELLANO.
A DIFFERENT WAY TO EXIST IN THE WORLD.

!
AND SHE KNEW WHAT SHE HAD TO DO.
?

BANG
BANG
IT'S TOMMY, LEMME IN.
HGGHH!
CRUNCH
IT WAS NEVER GOING TO BE A TEMPORARY THING. THEY WERE NEVER GOING BACK TO THEIR NORMAL LIVES.
KRAK
THEY WERE ALL IN THIS.
SKASSHH
ONE.
HUNDRED.
PERCENT.
KRACK

WHAT THE FUCK'VE YOU BEEN UP TO?
ONE-WAY STREET

THE '60s
KATH!
KATH! GET TOMMY ON THE PHONE!
BLEEDIN' 'ELL, KATH! GET HIM ON THE PHONE NOW. TELL HIM TO GET THE FUCK DOWN HERE!
DAD...
RAVEN, GO INTO YOUR ROOM, YOU DON'T NEED TO SEE THIS.
IS HE GOIN' TO DIE?
JUST GO, RAVEN!
YOU NEED TO GET DOWN HERE RIGHT NOW, TOMMY.

MARTIN, WHY ARE WE JUST WAITIN' AROUND? HE NEEDS A DOCTOR.
I KNOW, LOVE, BUT WE'VE GOT TO GET THIS SORTED FIRST. THEN WE'LL GET 'IM A DOCTOR, I PROMISE.
WHY DON'T YOU GO CHECK ON RAVEN--?
WHERE THE FUCK'VE YOU BEEN?
RELAX, MAN, ME AND JIMMY WERE JUST--
SMACK
I KNOW WHAT YOU'VE BEEN DOING, YOU DOPEY TWAT. STICKIN' THAT SHIT UP YOUR NOSE WHEN YOU SHOULD'VE BEEN HERE WITH US.
DAD, WHAT THE FUCK HAPPENED TO PADDY?
THAT FUCKIN' JEW SHYLOCK COHEN. HIM AND SOME OTHER FUCKING CUNTS ARE MAKIN' A MOVE ON US.

C'MON, YOU DON'T NEED TO SEE THIS.
YOU AN' JIMMY, YOU FIND COHEN AN' YOU FUCKIN' DO 'IM. YOU FUCKIN' DO 'IM HARD, OKAY?
CUT OFF HIS FUCKIN' HEAD AN' SEND IT TO THOSE OTHER FUCKS SO THEY KNOW WE'RE COMIN'.
YOU LISTENING TO ME, TOMMY? WE'RE GOIN' TO WAR WITH THESE JEW BASTARDS.
YEAH, DAD...
WHY DID THIS HAPPEN, JIMMY?
IT'S JUST A PART OF IT, KATH. PEOPLE GET HURT.
YOU GET USED TO IT. BLOOD DON'T SHOCK AFTER A WHILE.

NOW
TOMMY?
I HEARD ABOUT JIMMY AN THE GUYS AFT I GOT OUT, KATH.
MMMPPPHHH
BEEN HEARING A LOT ABOUT YOU THREE AS WELL. THOUGHT I SHOULD COME DOWN AND TALK.
HHHUUHH HHHELLPP HMMMMM
BUT THAT CAN WAIT 'TIL LATER.
SLAM
RIGHT NOW I NEED WHATEVER COOKIN' KNIVES YOU GOT, AND SOME GARBAGE BAGS.

ABATTOIR BLUES
THE ELBOW'S THE TOUGHEST PART. REAL BITCH TO HACK THROUGH.

"BUT BEFORE YOU DO THAT YOU GOTTA TAKE A SMALL KNIFE AND CUT ANYTHIN' IDENTIFYIN' OFF'A HIM.
"BIRTH MARKS. MOLES. TATTOOS. ALL THAT SHIT.
"THEN YOU CUT THE BODY INTO SMALL PIECES.
"YOU GOTTA MAKE SURE YOU PUNCTURE THE LUNGS AND STOMACH, OTHER-WISE THEY INFLATE IN THE WATER.
"AND YOU GET DEAD BODIES FLOATIN' 'ROUND MANHATTAN."
KRONEN'S DELICATESSEN

"IF YOU DO IT RIGHT, NO ONE'LL EVER FIND THE BODY. AND NO BODY MEANS NO INVESTIGATION."
SPLASH
WHAT NOW?
WE GET THE FUCK OUTTA HERE AND CLEAN UP THE BAR.
I MEAN WITH US.
WAY I SEE IT--
--I WORK WITH JIMMY. HE AIN'T HERE. YOU GIRLS SEEM TO BE DOIN' OKAY...
SO LOOKS LIKE I'M WORKIN' WITH YOU.

XXX
LIVE GIRLS!
EVERY WEEKNIGHT
WHAT THE FUCK IS THIS?
IT'S ALL I GOT.
YOU LYIN' TO ME, GIRL? YOU SKIMMIN' OFF THE TOP? STICKIN' MY MONEY IN YOUR ARM?
HEATHER?
PIZZA

IT WAS A FUCKIN' SLOW NIGHT. WHAT YOU GONNA DO?
THE RUNAWAYS
YOU GOTTA DRESS SEXY, GIRL. YOU LOOK LIKE A FUCKIN' BUM IN THEM RAGGEDY CLOTHES.
'LEAST I AIN'T DRESSED LIKE NO FAG.
WHAT THE FUCK YOU SAY TO ME?
I DIDN'T MEAN NOTHIN'.
WHAT THE FUCK'S GOIN' ON HERE?
STAY THE FUCK OUT'VE THIS, LADY.
KATH?
GET YOUR FUCKIN' HANDS OFFA HER.

THIS AIN'T OVER. I'LL FIND YOU.
CASEY'S PUB, CORNER OF 43RD. COME SEE IF I GIVE A FUCK.
YOU OKAY?
YEAH...
BUT WHAT THE FUCK, KATH? WHAT HAPPENED TO YOU?
I GUESS THINGS'VE CHANGED SINCE HIGH SCHOOL.
AIN'T THAT THE TRUTH.
D'YOU WANNA COME BACK TO THE BAR AND CLEAN YOURSELF UP?
YEAH, OKAY...

TIM'S WASH-N-DRY
TIM'S WASH-N-DRY
TIM'S WASH-N-DRY
TIM'S WASH-N-DRY
TIM'S WASH-N-DRY
DON'T MAKE ME FUCKIN' ASK FOR IT AGAIN, YOU FAT FUCK. I'LL CUT OUT YOUR FUCKIN' EYE-BALLS AND FILL THE HOLES WITH BLEACH.
N-DRY

WOULD YOU REALLY DO THAT?
FUCK NO, ANGIE. YOU SEEN WHAT BLEACH DOES TO YOUR CLOTHES?
...I'VE DONE SOME DISGUSTIN' SHIT IN THIS, BUT MOST TIMES YOU DON'T NEED TO. YOUR REPUTATION DOES MOST OF THE WORK.
OCCASIONALLY, THOUGH, SOME PEOPLE DO NEED REMINDIN'.
WHAT WAS IT LIKE IN THE ASYLUM?
YOU KNOW, YOU'RE THE FIRST PERSON WITH THE BALLS TO ASK ME THAT.
HALF THE TIME THEY HAD ME SO DOPED UP I COULD BARELY THINK, SO I DUNNO. IT IS WHAT IT IS, I GUESS.

I WAS PRETTY CRAZY WHEN I WENT IN. ME AND JIMMY WERE TEARIN' UP THE TOWN MOST NIGHTS, RAISIN' ALL KINDSA' HELL.
MAYBE IT WAS GOOD FOR ME, BEIN' IN THERE. I FEEL CALMER NOW.
LIKE I'D BE HAPPY JUST COLLECTIN' INSTEADA' ALL THE OTHER SHIT.
FUCK, MAYBE EVEN START A LEGIT BUSINESS.
OPEN A RESTAURANT OR SOMETHIN'. FIND A NICE ENGLISH GIRL LIKE MY DAD ALWAYS WANTED.
YOU GOIN' SOFT ON US, TOMMY?
NOT FUCKIN' YET. STILL GOT MORE HELL TO RAISE JUST GETTIN' YOUR OPERATION RUNNIN'.
LOANSHARKIN'S FINE, BUT YOU GOTTA THINK BIGGER IF YOU WANNA BRING IN SOME REAL DOUGH.
DO ANY OF YOU EVEN KNOW HOW TO CRACK A SAFE--?
SO YOU'RE GONNA START BRINGIN' HOOKERS BACK TO THE BAR NOW?!

GONNA TURN THE PLACE INTO A FUCKIN' BROTHEL?!?
IT'S HEATHER FROM HIGH SCHOOL FOR CHRIST'S SAKE!
WAS I MEANT TO LEAVE HER ON THE FUCKIN' STREET?!
YES! SHE'S A FUCKIN' WHORE! IT'S WHERE SHE BELONGS--
SMACK
WHAT THE FUCK WAS THAT ABOUT?

HEY!
YOU RAVEN?
YEAH...
YEAH, OKAY, WE'VE BOTH GOT ONE. I JUST WANT TO TALK, NOT HAVE A SHOOT-OUT IN THE STREET.
WHAT ABOUT?
I WANNA TALK ABOUT HOW THREE HOUSEWIVES ARE NOW CONTROLLIN' ALL THE LOAN-SHARKIN' RACKETS IN HELL'S KITCHEN.

WHO THE FUCK ARE YOU?
MY NAME'S TONY. I'M WITH ALFONSO GARGANO. OUT IN QUEENS.
YOU'VE BEEN BUSY SINCE YOUR HUSBANDS GOT PINCHED, AIN'T YOU? I KNOW YOU KILLED NICKY AN' YOU GOT THAT PSYCHO TOMMY WORKIN' FOR YOU--
I THINK YOU'VE GOT THE WRONG GIRL, TONY. I DON'T KNOW NO NICKY.
C'MON, RAVEN, DON' BULLSHIT ME. A COUPLA' GUYS SAW 'IM GOIN' INTO CASEY'S AFTER HOURS. NO ONE'S SEEN 'IM SINCE.
TOMMY WAS ALWAYS GOOD AT DOIN' THAT HOUDINI ACT ONNA' CORPSE.
YOU KNOW, IT TOOK A LOTTA PERSUADIN' TO EVEN FIND THAT OUT. PEOPLE 'ROUND HERE GOT A LOTTA RESPECT FOR YOU GIRLS.
YOU MEAN THEY RESPECT OUR HUSBANDS.
NO, I MEAN YOU. IT DON' HURT YOU GOT TOMMY...
BUT THESE DAYS WHEN THEY SAY BRENNAN'S CREW, THEY DON' MEAN JIMMY.

I GOT SOME WORK WE MIGHT BE ABLE TO DO TOGETHER. IF YOU AN' KATH ARE INTERESTED.
THAT'S THE NUMBER FOR A PAY-PHONE. THERE'LL BE SOMEONE THERE TWO 'TIL FIVE EVERY OTHER DAY.
A PAYPHONE? HOW COME YOU DON'T HAVE AN OFFICE, LIKE IN THE GODFATHER?
I MAY BE AS GOOD-LOOKIN' AS MICHAEL CORLEONE, BUT LIFE AIN'T THE SAME AS THE MOVIES.
DON'T FLATTER YOURSELF, TONY. YOU'RE CUTE, BUT YOU AIN'T PACINO.
CALL THE NUMBER, I'LL ARRANGE THE SITDOWN WITH GARGANO AN' WE'LL SEE WHAT WE CAN WORK OUT.
IF YOU WANT, WE CAN MEET UP BEFORE. HAVE SOME FOOD, TALK IT OVER.
HITTIN' ON A GIRL WHEN HER HUSBAND'S IN PRISON. AIN'T THERE SOME MAFIOSO CODE AGAINST THAT?

THIS AIN'T SOME TRAP, IS IT? GET REVENGE FOR TAKIN' OUT ONE OF YOUR PEOPLE?
WHO, NICKY? HE WAS A TWO-BIT HUSTLER AN' A SCUMBAG. HE WASN'T CONNECTED.
HONESTLY, YOU DID ME A FAVOR. I THINK HE GOT MY BROTHER INTO SOME SHIT A WHILE BACK.
YOUR BROTHER?
YEAH, FRANKY. THE BLACK SHEEP OF THE CASTELLANO FAMILY. SOME FUCK PUT 'IM INNA COMA.
I DON' KNOW WHO DID IT, BUT I KNOW THAT FUCK NICKY WAS INVOLVED.
ANYWAY, ENOUGH DWELLIN' ON THE BAD SHIT IN LIFE. WHAT'S THAT IRISH WORD YOU GOT FOR THAT?
MAUDLIN?
YEAH... ENOUGH MAUDLIN...
CALL ME!

FOR FUCK'S SAKE, C'MON.
KATH!
WHERE ARE YOU?--
KATH, I'M NOT SURE, BUT WE COULD BE SERIOUSLY FUCKED. I JUST HAD A VISIT FROM TONY CASTELLANO.
ABOUT FRANKY? DOES HE KNOW IT WAS US?
NO...I DUNNO.
HE COULD BE FUCKIN' WITH US, BUT I DON'T THINK HE IS. HE KNOWS WE TOOK OUT NICKY, BUT DIDN'T CONNECT US TO FRANKY.

WHAT DID HE WANT, THEN?
HE WANTS US TO HAVE A SITDOWN WITH GARGANO. THINKS WE COULD DO BUSINESS TOGETHER.
REALLY? SHIT, IF WE CAN GET CONNECTED WITH GARGANO, JIMMY WON'T BE ABLE TO TOUCH US.
JIMMY?
I JUST GOT OFF THE PHONE WITH JIMMY'S LAWYER. THERE'S BEEN SOME NEW DEVELOPMENT OR SOMETHIN'.
THEY'RE GONNA BE OUT IN A FEW MONTHS.
LOOKS LIKE WE'VE GOTTA GET OUR SHIT TOGETHER.

ROB
THEY WERE AT A HIGH SCHOOL PARTY.
SOME GUY GRABBED HER ASS, SO ROB BEAT THE SHIT OUT OF HIM.
WHEN SHE ASKED HIM WHY HE DID IT, HE SAID:
"YOU JUST DON'T TREAT A LADY LIKE THAT."
NIEW
SHE KISSED HIM ON THE CHEEK AS A THANK YOU AND HE FELL HOPELESSLY IN LOVE WITH HER.
ROB?
ANGIE, BABY! YOU CHANGED THE LOCKS?
SHE FELT SO SAFE WITH HIM. AND SHE WANTED TO LOVE HIM FOR MAKING HER FEEL LIKE THAT.
DIDN'T THINK YOU WERE OUT 'TIL TOMORROW.

BUT SHE DIDN'T...
THE LAWYER GOT US OUT EARLY. WE DIDN'T SAY NOTHIN'.
WE THOUGHT IT'D BE A NICE SURPRISE.
GOT ANY OTHER FUCKIN' SURPRISES?
ANGIE?
GIMME YOUR GUN, ROB.
I AIN'T GOT A GUN, FOR CHRIST'S SAKE. WHY WOULD I HAVE A GUN?
STOP FUCKIN' AROUND. JIMMY SENT YOU HERE, DIDN'T HE?
ANGIE, PLEASE... JIMMY DIDN'T SEND ME HERE. I CAME HERE 'COZ I MISSED YOU.
I KNOW THERE'S BEEN SOME SHIT GOIN' ON SINCE WE WENT AWAY.
BUT I FIGURED, NOW I'M OUT, THINGS'D JUST GO BACK TO HOW IT WAS BEFORE.
FOR CHRIST'S SAKE, YOU'VE GOT NO IDEA, DO YOU?
I'M SORRY, ROB, BUT IT'S NEVER GONNA BE HOW IT WAS BEFORE.
SHE DIDN'T LOVE HIM. BUT HE'D MEANT ENOUGH TO ANGIE THAT, IF THE TIME CAME...
...SHE DIDN'T WANT TO BE THE ONE WHO WOULD HAVE TO KILL HIM.

HOMECOMIN'
SPIN!
ROZE'S
ROZE'S DELICAT
P

ONE WEEK BEFORE RELEASE.
OY GEVALT! WHAT THESE GIRLS WEAR TODAY!
IT'S A NEW ERA, HERB. THE TIMES CHANGE, AND SO SHOULD WE.
SO...WHAT DO YOU THINK OF MY PROPOSITION?
FEH! WORKING WITH THOSE IRISH DOGS. WOMEN AS WELL! WHO LETS THEIR WOMAN DO THIS WORK?
I DON'T KNOW, HERB...
"THEY'VE BEEN DOING WELL THESE LAST FEW MONTHS. MAKING A LOT OF MONEY."
YES...BUT THESE WOMEN WOULD BE NOTHING WITHOUT THAT MESHUGENAH TOMMY.

YOU'RE NOT PAYING ENOUGH ATTENTION, HERB.
"I CAN SEE SOMETHING IN KATH AND RAVEN. THEY'VE BEEN MAKING SOME SERIOUS MOVES.
"YOU KNOW THEY'RE HAVING A SIT-DOWN WITH GARGANO?"
GARGANO?
"THEY'RE SMART GIRLS. AND THE OTHER ONE, ANGIE. WELL...
"LET'S JUST SAY TOMMY HAS BEEN TEACHING HER SOME OF HIS UNIQUE SKILLS."

AH, YOU SEE! SAME AS THEIR HUSBANDS, ALL FISTS AND GUNS.
THE IRISH DON'T HAVE THE BRAINS FOR REAL BUSINESS.
BUT THEY'RE NOT THEIR HUSBANDS, HERB.
"THEY REBUILT THEIR FATHER'S RELATIONSHIP AT FEATHERSTONE'S.
"HIJACKING, NO-SHOW JOBS, KICKBACKS. SHYLOCKING TO THE DRIVERS AND WARE-HOUSE WORKERS."
YOU DON'T GET THESE THINGS WITH VIOLENCE ALONE.

BUT, LARRY, IF I MAKE A DEAL WITH THEM--
"--WHAT DEAL DO I HAVE WHEN THEIR HUSBANDS RETURN? AND THEY GO BACK TO JUST BEING HOUSEWIVES?
"I DON'T WANT TO END UP LIKE COHEN."
I'M SORRY, LARRY. YOU'RE A GOOD BOY, BUT THIS JUST ISN'T FOR ME.
I'M SORRY TOO, HERB.
IT TOOK A LOT TO PERSUADE THEM ON YOU.
AFTER ALL THAT BAD BLOOD WITH YOU AND TOMMY'S FATHER...HE WAS JUST LOOKING FOR A REASON.

BLAM
THIS IS THE PROBLEM WITH OUR BUSINESS.
EVEN WITH A GUN TO OUR HEAD WE REFUSE TO MOVE FORWARD.
TELL KATH AND RAVEN I'M READY TO DO BUSINESS NOW.

I'M SURE THEY'LL BE REALLY FUCKIN' PLEASED.
SKREEETCH
I LIKE THESE GIRLS.

JOHNNY
YOU BETTER GET OUTTA HERE. KATH'S COMIN' OVER SOON.
AN' YOU DON' WANNA BE SEEN WITH NO DIRTY WOP?
YOU KNOW HOW IT IS...
YEAH, I KNOW.
I'M JUST YOUR FLOOZY ON THE SIDE.
YOU KNOW IT AIN'T LIKE THAT. I LIKE YOU, TONY, AND THIS FEELS RIGHT.
IT'S JUST, IT'S DIFFICULT RIGHT NOW.
YEAH, I KNOW.
I'M A BIG BOY. I CAN WAIT FOR YOU TO GET THINGS STRAIGHT WITH EVERYONE--
KNOCK KNOCK
THAT'LL BE KATH, YOU BETTER HIDE.
IT WAS JUST A DRUNKEN ONE-NIGHT STAND WHEN SHE WAS HOME FROM HER FRESHMAN YEAR AT COLLEGE.

LATER, THEY FOUND OUT SHE WAS TWO MONTHS PREGNANT.
THEY WERE MARRIED BEFORE THEY KNEW SHE'D LOST THE CHILD.
YOU CHANGED THE FUCKIN' LOCKS?
YOU TRYIN' TO KEEP ME OUTTA MY OWN HOME?
YOU THINK NOW YOU'RE QUEEN OF FUCKIN' HELL'S KITCHEN THAT THIS IS ALL YOURS?
CATHOLIC GUILT KEPT THEM FROM DIVORCING, BUT THERE WAS NO LOVE THERE.
FUCKIN' DISGRACIN' OUR NAME OUT THERE--
GET YOUR FUCKIN' HANDS OFFA' HER!
WHO THE FUCK IS THIS GUY?
AND WHAT THE FUCK'RE YOU DOIN' WITH MY WIFE?
KLIK

SHE RESENTED HIM FOR NOT LETTING HER GO BACK TO COLLEGE.
DROP THE KNIFE.
HE RESENTED HER FOR NOT BEING ABLE TO GIVE HIM A SON.
AND THAT HAD BEEN THEIR LIFE.
WHAT THE FUCK, RAVEN?
JUST GO, JOHNNY.
THIS AIN'T FUCKIN' OVER.
YES IT IS IT. WAS OVER LONG BEFORE YOU WENT AWAY. WE JUST NEVER SAID IT.
I WON' LET HIM HURT YOU.
I DON'T NEED YOU TO FUCKIN' SAVE ME, TONY.

ONE WEEK BEFORE RELEASE.
HOW'D IT GO?
HERB DIDN'T TAKE THE OFFER.
AND I'M SURE YOU WERE REALLY DISAPPOINTED WITH THAT, TOMMY.
ROYAL

YOU EVER DONE BUSINESS WITH THESE GUYS, TOMMY?
GARGANO? NAH. I DEALT WITH WISEGUYS BEFORE, THOUGH.
I COULD NEVER GET WITH ALL THAT ASS-KISSING, MAFIA CODE CRAP.
IT'S ALL BULLSHIT. THEY'RE ALWAYS SCREWIN' EACH OTHER OVER AND KILLIN' EACH OTHER WITHOUT THE BIG BOSS'S SAY-SO.
DO A DEAL WITH HIM, YEAH. BUT DON'T EVER FUCKIN' TRUST HIM.
IF SCREWIN' YOU HELPS HIM, HE'LL SCREW YOU.
MATRANGA'S MUSICAL INSTRUMENTS
I'D STILL FEEL BETTER IF YOU CAME IN WITH US.
IT'S YOUR THING, NOT MINE. YOU DON'T NEED ME.

REMEMBER, JUST 'CAUSE YOU AIN'T GOT A DICK DON'T MEAN YOU GOTTA BE TREATED LIKE ONE.
DON'T TAKE NO SHIT.
MATRANGA'S
MUSICAL INSTRUMEN
HOW IS THAT CRAZY FUCK STILL ALIVE?

LADIES! TAKE A SEAT.
IT'S AN HONOR TO MEET YOU, MR. GARGANO.
SONNY, GO GET SOME COFFEE FOR EVERYONE.
SLURP

IT'S KATH, RAVEN AN' ANGIE, RIGHT?
UH, YEAH.
SO TELL ME, KATH, RAVEN AN' ANGIE. WHY THE FUCK'M I TALKIN' TO YOU?
AL, I SPOKE TO YOU ABOUT THEM--
NO, TONY. I WANT THEM TO EXPLAIN WHY I'M HAVIN' A SIT-DOWN WITH THREE MICK TWATS FROM HELL'S KITCHEN.
BECAUSE NOW WE'RE TOO BIG TO IGNORE.
WE GOT CONNECTIONS WITH FEATHERSTONE TRUCKIN'. WE CONTROL THE SHYLOCK AND NUMBERS IN HELL'S KITCHEN.
AND WE'RE THE ONLY CONNECTION YOU HAVE WITH RABBI JACOBS' CREW.
THE RABBI DON' HAVE A CREW. HE WORKS FOR HERB TEMKIN.
NOT SINCE ANGIE PUT BULLET IN THE BACK OF HERB HEAD EARLIE TODAY.

OKAY. IF I MAKE A DEAL WITH YOU, AM I MAKIN' A DEAL WITH YOUR HUSBANDS, AS WELL?
NO. JUST WITH US. THEY'RE OUR PROBLEM, NOT YOURS.
GOOD. THEY WEREN'T BUSINESSMEN. TOO WILD. YOU NEVER KNEW WHAT THEY'D DO NEXT.
WHAT ABOUT TOMMY?
WHAT ABOUT HIM?
HE'S BEEN GOOD FOR YOU. GAVE YOU CREDIBILITY. WHAT YOU GONNA DO IF HE GOES BACK TO JIMMY?
TOMMY'S BEEN GOOD FOR US, YEAH, AND I DON'T THINK HE WOULD GO WITH THEM.
BUT IF HE DOES...
ANGIE'LL PUT A BULLET IN THE BACK OF HIS HEAD.
KATH, ANGIE. IF I WAS YOU, I'D STICK WITH THIS ONE.
EIGHT PERCENT OF YOUR EARNIN'S GETS YOU MY PROTECTION. WE'LL HAVE SOME REAL WORK COMIN' UP AS WELL.
NOW, ENOUGH BUSINESS, LET'S DRINK TO NEW FRIENDSHIPS.

JIMMY
SHE LOVED HIM.
SINCE THE FIRST DAY THEY MET, SHE'D LOVED HIM.
THIS DON'T HAVE TO HAPPEN.
AND, IN WHATEVER CAPACITY HE HAD FOR EMOTION... HE LOVED HER AS WELL.

YOU GONNA LET US KEEP EARNIN'?
BUT SHE KNEW THEY COULDN'T GO BACK TO WHAT THEY'D HAD BEFORE.
THEN, YEAH...
...IT **DOES** HAVE TO HAPPEN.

WANNA SPLIT IT NOW?
YEAH.
LOVE, LIES & BULLETS
DRINK?
JUST ONE, I GOTTA GET BACK TO THE KIDS.
HEATHER'S GOTTA CAR BOOKED FOR TWELVE.

YOU GOT THAT FUCKIN' JUNKIE LOOKIN' AFTER YOUR KIDS?
SHE'S CLEAN NOW. AIN'T TOUCHED THAT SHIT INNA MONTH.

JUNKIES NEVER CHANGE...
GIVE HER A BREAK, RAVEN, SHE'S TRYIN' TO GET HERSELF RIGHT.

SHE STILL HOOKIN'?

YEAH...
SHE SAYS SHE'S GONNA GIVE IT UP WHEN SHE GETS ENOUGH MONEY TO GO BACK TO COLLEGE.
I GO DOWN TIMES SQUARE WITH HER SOMETIMES. MAKE SURE PEOPLE KNOW NOT TO FUCK WITH HER.
WHAT PERCENTAGE YOU GETTIN' FOR THAT?
I'M NOT.
YOU'RE NOT TAKIN' A FUCKIN' CUT? WE'RE RUNNIN' A BUSINESS HERE, NOT A CHARITY!
FOR FUCK'S SAKE! SHE'S A FRIEND WHO NEEDS MY HELP!
YOU START THINKIN' OF THESE PEOPLE AS FRIENDS, KATH, WE'RE NEVER GONNA MAKE ANY FUCKIN' MONEY.
AFTER ALL THE SHIT YOU GAVE ME ABOUT RUNNIN' GIRLS, YOU WANNA TAX HEATHER?
YOU GIVE HER PROTECTION, SHE GIVES YOU A CUT. IT'S WHAT WE DO.
WE GONNA STOP COLLECTIN' EVERY TIME SOMEONE'S GOTTA FUCKIN' SOB STORY?
WHERE'S YOUR HEART, RAVEN?

DON'T GO SOFT ON ME, KATH.
YOU KNOW, YOU'RE TALKIN' PRETTY FUCKIN' BIG FOR SOME-ONE WHO DIDN'T EVEN WANNA GET INTO THIS.
YEAH, BUT WE'RE FUCKIN' IN IT NOW, AIN'T WE? AND IF WE'RE GONNA DO IT, WE GOTTA DO IT RIGHT.
IF YOU CAN'T SEE THAT ANYMORE, MAYBE YOU SHOULD JUST GET OUTTA THIS THING. BEFORE THAT BIG FUCKIN' HEART OF YOURS BREAKS.
OH, FUCK YOU IF YOU BELIEVE THAT, RAVEN.
EVEN IN THIS, SOME THINGS ARE MORE IMPORTANT THAN MONEY.
SLAM

HEY, TOMMY!
ROB! I HEARD YOU GOT OUT EARLY.
FUCK, TOMMY, YOU STILL DOIN' THAT SHIT?
I THOUGHT YOU QUIT THE JUNK.
JUST COLLECTIN' MAN. JUST COLLECTIN.'
THAT'S GOOD, 'CAUSE THAT SHIT USED TO FUCK YOU UP.

IT'S GOOD TO SEE YOU!
WE HAVIN' A REUNION OR WHAT? WHERE'S JIMMY AND JOHNNY?
THEY COULDN'T MAKE IT...
HOW YOU BEEN?
GETTIN' BY, SAME AS ALWAYS.
YEAH...
HEARD YOU BEEN WORKIN' WITH THE GIRLS.
YEAH, BEEN HELPIN' THEM OUT 'TIL I GET MY OWN THING GOIN'.
YOU REALLY THINK THIS IS A GOOD LINE OF WORK FOR WOMEN?
YOU REALLY THINK THAT'S OUR FUCKIN' CHOICE TO MAKE, ROB?

ENOUGH OF THIS SHIT, TOMMY, WHO YOU WITH? US OR THEM?
I DIDN'T KNOW I HAD TO PICK A SIDE.
OF COURSE YOU FUCKIN' DO!
WHAT YOU GONNA DO, TOMMY? TURN ON YOUR CREW AS WELL AS FUCK MY WIFE?
WHAT!? I AIN'T FUCKIN' ANGIE!
DON'T YOU FUCKIN' LIE TO ME! EVERY-ONE'S SEEN YOU TOGETHER.
YOU'RE THE SAME AS THAT FUCKIN' GREASEBALL CASTELLANO.
LOOK, ROB, I AIN'T LYING. ANGIE'S LIKE A SISTER--
CRAKK

GET THE FUCK OFFA ME!
GET YOUR FUCKIN' HANDS OFFA ME!

SO TONY DIDN'T SAY WHAT WAS IN THE TRUCK?
IT'S NONE'VE OUR FUCKIN' BUSINESS, KATH, HE JUST TOLD US A TIME ANNA' PLACE.
IT MAKES A FUCKIN' DIFFERENCE IN HOW MUCH PRISON TIME WE GET IF IT GOES TO SHIT.
HOW MANY GOONS'RE GONNA BE IN THE TRUCK?
SHOULD JUST BE THE DRIVER.
ARMED?
YEAH, KEEPS A SHOTGUN ON THE PASSENGER SEAT.
WE'RE STEALIN' FROM ANOTHER CREW.
WHAT?
WHY'S HE GOTTA GUN IF HE'S JUST A REGULAR TRUCK DRIVER? THE CARGO AIN'T WORTH HIS LIFE.
BUT IF HE'S GOTTA FUCKIN' ANSWER TO MR. "I'LL CUT YOUR BALLS OFF IF YA' FUCK WITH ME" GOOMBAH DON, HE'S GOTTA STAKE IN PROTECTIN' IT.
IT'S WHY GARGANO'S USIN' US. HE DON'T WANNA BE SEEN TO BE INVOLVED IN HITTIN' ANOTHER CREW--
NEW YO
MANHATTAN
BRONX
Pelham

HEY...
WHAT THE FUCK, TOMMY? I'VE BEEN TRYIN' TO CALL YOU.
WHAT HAPPENED?
NONE'VE YOUR FUCKIN' BUSINESS.
WE STILL ON FOR TONIGHT?
YEAH...
GOOD, 'CAUSE WE'RE GONNA NEED THE ITALIANS WITH US IN THIS.
JIMMY'S GOT SOME LOCAL GUYS WITH HIM NOW, NOT JUST JOHNNY AND ROB.
WE GET TIGHT WITH GARGANO--
THEN WE GO TO FUCKIN' WAR.

SO, HOW LONG YOU BEEN FUCKIN' TONY FOR?
WHAT?
C'MON, RAVEN, YOU AIN'T EXACTLY DISCREET. I KNOW ALL ABOUT IT.
YOU DO, HUH? I DON'T REMEMBER IT BEING ANY OF YOUR FUCKIN' BUSINESS.
JESUS, RAVEN, I DON'T CARE ABOUT YOU CHEATIN' ON JOHNNY. I JUST WANTED TO TALK.
I FEEL LIKE WE'RE MOVIN' APART...
MAYBE I JUST DON'T FUCKIN' WANNA TALK ABOUT IT. DID YOU EVER THINK OF THAT?
AND WHEN DID YOU EVER GIVE A FUCK BEFORE ABOUT US MOVIN' APART?
HONK HONK HOOOOOON
HEY! GET OUTTA THE ROAD!

OUR CAR'S BROKEN DOWN, CAN YOU HELP US OUT?
SORRY, LADY, I GOT PLACES TO BE.
CHUNK
KLIK
GET OUTTA THE FUCKIN' TRUCK.

OLIVE OIL CO.
OPEN THE FUCKIN' DOORS. I WANNA SEE WHAT WE'RE FUCKIN' STEALIN'.
AH, FUCK...
OKAY, I'M OPENING THE DOOR NOW. IT'S ME, PAULIE, OPENING THE DOOR.
?
OLIVE OIL CO.
KLIK
BLAM
OLIVE OIL CO.

BLAM
BLAMBLAM
BLAM BLAM
BLAM BLAM
KLIK
KLIK
FUCK.
ZO'D
OIL CO.

BLAM

FUCK YEAH, ANGIE!
TOMMY, YOU AND ANGIE DUMP THE PICKUP, THEN COME BACK FOR THE TRUCK. WE'LL TAKE THE BUG.

KNOCK
KNOCK
KNOCK
HEY!
I'VE GOT A PRESENT FOR YOU.
IT'S NOT PARKED OUTSIDE, IS IT?
IT'S OVER AT FEATHERSTONE'S WAITING FOR ONE OF YOUR GUYS TO PICK IT UP.
I HELPED MYSELF TO ONE OF THE COATS. I HOPE YOU DON'T MIND.
NAH... IT LOOKS GOOD ON--

WHAT?
NOTHIN'...
C'MON, **WHAT?**
RAVEN, I THINK I LOVE YOU...

MUSICAL INSTRUME
HEY, JIMMY...
HE'LL SEE YA.
SO, JIMMY. TELL ME WHY I SHOULDN'T JUST GET SONNY HERE TO CUT YOUR THROAT RIGHT NOW.
I AIN'T GOT NO PROBLEM WITH YOU.
SMAK
NO, BUT YOU GOTTA PROBLEM WITH YOUR WIFE'S CREW, WHO'RE UNDER MY PROTECTION.
THOSE GIRLS'RE MAKIN' ME MONEY. YOU'RE LOOKIN' TO STOP THAT BY TAKIN' 'EM OUTTA ACTION.
YOU SEE WHAT I'M SAYIN' HERE, RIGHT? YOU DUMB IRISH FUCK. DO YOU SEE NOW WHY IT WAS A BAD IDEA COMIN' HERE?

FUCK, WHY'M I EVEN TALKIN' TO YA?
JUST FUCKIN' KILL HIM ALREADY, I AIN'T GOT ALL DAY.
WAIT! I CAME HERE TO MAKE A FUCKIN' DEAL!
YEAH? WHAT KINDA DEAL?
LET ME TAKE OVER KATH'S RACKETS. YOU'LL GET THE SAME MONEY COMIN' IN, YOU'LL JUST DEAL WITH ME INSTEADA' HER.
IT CAN'T BE GOOD FOR YOUR REPUTATION WORKIN' WITH A CREW FULLA WOMEN.
ME, THOUGH? I'VE GOT A REPUTATION PEOPLE KNOW ABOUT.
YEAH, YOU CERTAINLY GOTTA REPUTATION...
BUT SO HAVE I. AN' IF I BREAK MY WORD, THEN WHAT'S MY REPUTATION WORTH? WHERE'S THE HONOR IN THAT?
SO IF THAT'S ALL YOU GOT, THEN...
IS IT HONORABLE FOR ONE OF YOUR GUYS TO FUCK SOME-ONE ELSE'S WIFE?

YOUR GUY TONY, HE'S FUCKIN' RAVEN.
YOU KNOW, I'VE NEVER LIKED THAT GUY. THINKS HE'S BETTER THAN EVERYONE ELSE WITHOUT EARNIN' IT.
YOU CAN'T TRUST A GUY LIKE THAT.
YOU GET RAVEN'S HUSBAND TO WHACK TONY, MAKE IT LOOK LIKE AN HONOR THING. KEEP ME OUT'VE IT.
YOU DO THAT AN' I'LL STAY OUTTA YOUR WAY WITH THIS BUSINESS WITH KATH.
BUT JIMMY, IF ANYONE EVER FUCKIN' HEARS I HAD ANYTHIN' TO DO WITH MADE GUY GETTIN WHACKED--
--WE WON'T KILL YA BEFORE WE CUT YA UP FOR THE RIVER...

RADIO TALK
30

42 PROOF
AAHHHHHH

WELL, IT'S ONE WAY TO SEND A FUCKIN' MESSAGE.
GET HIM OFF THE STREET.
I DON'T WANNA SEE THIS RIGHT NOW.
WHAT WE DO TO SURVIVE
WHAT D'YOU THINK THEY DID WITH HIS HEAD?
I PICKED A SIDE

TOMMY, WHAT THE FUCK IS THAT?
ROB'S HEAD.
YOU'RE FUCKIN' KIDDIN'!
WHERE'S THE REST OF HIM?
I LEFT HIM IN FRONT OF JIMMY'S PLACE--
AH, SHIT...

ANGIE, I'M SORRY. I DIDN'T THINK YOU WERE HERE.
NO... IT'S OKAY...I JUST WASN'T EXPECTIN'...
WHAT THE FUCK'S THAT?
THAT?
THAT'S TOMMY, STARTIN' A FUCKIN' **WAR.**

BANG BANG BANG BANG
KRAK

WHERE IS HE?!

HE'S NOT FUCKIN' HERE, JOHNNY!

IF HE'S NOT HERE THEN WHERE THE FUCK IS HE?
GET OUTTA HERE!
YOU CHEATIN' FUCKIN' WHORE YOU THINK YOU CAN JUST...
AH FUCK, RAVEN...
WHY COULDN'T YOU'VE JUST BEEN GOOD TO ME? ALL I EVER WANTED WAS A WIFE AND KIDS...
INSTEAD I GOT YOU.

WHY HIM?
DO YOU LOVE HIM?
IT DON'T FUCKIN' MATTER ANYWAY, HE'LL BE DEAD SOON.
WHAT?
THAT WOP FUCK GARGANO. HE'S GOT A HARD-ON FOR TONY, BUT MADE GUYS AIN'T MEANT TO KILL EACH OTHER.
SO WE WHACK HIM AND GARGANO BACKS US INSTEAD'A YOU...

GET OFFA ME!
RING RING
RING RING
RING RING
RING RING
RING RING
RING RING RING RING

BLAM
RING RING
RING RING
RING RING
RING RING
RING RING
RING RING
RING RING
RING RING
RING RING
RING RING
RING RING
RING RING
RING RING

WHAT!?
FRANKY CASTELLANO HAD COME OUT OF HIS COMA.
HE WASN'T TALKING YET BUT THE DOCTORS (AND THE COPS) WERE HOPEFUL.
SO IT WAS ONLY A MATTER OF TIME.
RAVEN SURPRISED HERSELF BY KNOWING EXACTLY WHAT TO DO.
AFTER SHE GOT OFF THE PHONE WITH KATH, SHE CALLED TOMMY TO GET RID OF JOHNNY'S BODY AND MAKE SURE THE NEIGHBORS WEREN'T GOING TO TALK.

THEN SHE MADE HER WAY OVER TO QUEENS.

WHY THE FUCK D'YOU IRISH NEVER CALL FIRST?
I KNOW YOU MADE A DEAL WITH JIMMY.
TAKE A SEAT.
SO, WHAT D'YOU KNOW? DID JIMMY FUCKIN' SQUEAL ON ME?
NO, MY HUSBAND TOLD ME...
RIGHT BEFORE I SHOT HIM.

OKAY, SO YOU KNOW. WHAT NOW?
I WANNA MAKE A DEAL WITH YOU.
YEAH, WHAT KINDA DEAL?
KLIK
I'LL GET RID'VE TONY IF YOU KILL HIS BROTHER FRANKY.

WHY D'YOU WANT FRANKY?
HEHEHE. IT WAS YOU GIRLS THAT FUCKED HIM UP...
WITH YOUR CONNECTIONS, CAN YOU GET TO FRANKY? BEFORE HE TALKS TO TONY OR THE COPS?
SURE, I GOT PEOPLE IN THE HOSPITAL...BUT CAN YOU GUARANTEE TONY'S DEATH DON'T COME BACK ON ME?
YES.
THEN WE'VE GOT A FUCKIN' DEAL.

"BUT FROM NOW ON, IN THIS THING, I ONLY TALK TO YOU. KATH TALKS BIG, BUT SHE AIN'T GOT THE HEART FOR IT.
"BUT YOU, RAVEN. YOU WERE BORN TO DO THIS."

RAVEN? WHAT THE FUCK'VE YOU DONE TO YOUR HAIR?
I JUST NEEDED A CHANGE...YOU OKAY?
YEAH, I'M FINE. JUST SOME FAMILY BUSINESS.
YOU WANNA COME IN? I'LL TELL YOU ABOUT IT.
YEAH, OKAY.

YOU TREATED ME BETTER THAN ANY-ONE ELSE, TONY.
BLAM

HHHHGGHH

NINE ONE ONE. WHAT IS THE NATURE OF YOUR EMERGENCY?
I JUST SAW TWO PUERTO RICAN GUYS SHOOT SOMEONE--

Casey's

-- SO IT LOOKS LIKE THIS HEAT WAVE IS GOING TO BE WITH US FOR A WHILE LONGER.
THANK YOU, JENNIFER. NOW TONIGHT ON WPIX, A CITY UNDER SIEGE AS THE MYSTERIOUS KILLER, NOW KNOWN AS SON OF SAM, IS STILL AT LARGE DESPITE--
!
THE GIRLS FROM HELL'S KITCHEN SAY HELLO, FRANKY.
UUUMMMMPPPHHHH
WHAT THE FUCK?

EVERY-
THING
GOES TO
HELL

SEE IF YOU CAN FIND A WORKING PAYPHONE AND TELL KATH WE'LL MEET HER AT CASEY'S WITH RAVEN.
OKAY...
HOW YOU DOIN', TOMMY?
ME? I'M FINE.
YEAH? 'CAUSE YOU'VE BEEN HITTIN' IT PRETTY HARD LATELY.
YEAH, I GUESS...THIS WHOLE THING'S JUST GOT ME RATTLED, YOU KNOW? JIMMY'S LIKE A BROTHER TO ME...
I DUNNO. WE'VE ALL BEEN THROUGH SOME SHIT, ANGIE--

"--YOU GOTTA EXPECT IT TO FUCK YOU UP A LITTLE..."
HEY.
I LIKE THE NEW LOOK. SUITS YOU.
THANKS...
THIS BLACK-OUT'S FUCKIN' SOMETHIN', AIN'T IT?
YEAH, IT'S GETTIN' CRAZY OUT THERE.
WE'RE ALL HEADIN' DOWN TO THE BAR TO HOLD UP 'TIL IT BLOWS OVER--
YOU OKAY, RAVEN?

WHEN DID IT ALL BECOME NORMAL, TOMMY? GUNS AND FUCKIN' HEADS IN BOWLIN' BAGS?
WHEN DID THAT BECOME OUR LIVES?
I DUNNO IF IT'S EVER NORMAL. IT'S JUST SHIT YOU DO TO GET BY.
JUST SHIT WE DO...I NEVER THOUGHT THIS WOULD BE SHIT WE JUST DO.
BUT THE FUCKED-UP THING IS THAT THE MORE WE GET INTO IT...
YOU KNOW WHAT GARGAND SAID TO ME? HE SAID I WAS BORN TO DO THIS.
FUCK, AFTER EVERYTHIN' I'VE DONE. MAYBE HE'S RIGHT.
WITH DADS LIKE OURS, THE WAY WE GREW UP? WE NEVER HAD A CHANCE AT A NORMAL LIFE, DID WE?

YEAH, MY FUCKIN' FATHER.
YOU SEE, YOU HAD A FUCKIN' GANGSTER SAINT FOR A DAD. A CRIMINAL WITH A HEART OF GOLD AND ALL THAT SHIT.
MY DAD WAS A FUCKIN' CUNT WIFE BEATER WHO CARED MORE ABOUT HIS BUSINESS THAN HIS FAMILY.
KATH COULD NEVER SEE IT, SHE IGNORED ALL TH BAD SHIT. BUT ALWAYS SAW HI FOR WHAT HE WAS.
DID SHE EVER TELL YOU HOW MOM GOT HER SCARS?
I HEARD RUMORS...
WHEN ALL THAT SHIT WAS HAPPENING WITH THE PUERTO RICANS. TWO GUYS FOUND MOM AT WORK AND BEAT THE SHIT OUT OF HER--
--AS A WARNING TO MY DAD.
THAT FUCK. HE DIDN'T CARE THAT SHE WAS HURT. HE WAS JUST PISSED THEY'D MADE A MOVE AGAINST HIM.
HE DIDN'T VISIT HER ONCE IN THE FUCKIN' HOSPITAL. HE WAS OUT ON THE STREETS GETTIN' HIS REVENGE.

THE GUYS WHO DID IT...
THEY DIDN'T GIVE A FUCK ABOUT HER EITHER. THEY MIGHT AS WELL'VE BEEN FUCKING UP HIS CAR FOR ALL SHE MEANT TO THEM.
OUR MOM NEVER LIVED HER OWN LIFE. SHE JUST LIVED IN THE BACKGROUND OF OUR DAD'S.
I AIN'T GONNA BE LIKE THAT, TOMMY. I DON'T CARE WHAT I HAVE TO DO OR WHO I HAVE TO FUCKIN' KILL--
BANG BANG BANG
JIMMY'S TAKEN THE FUCKIN' KIDS!
GUYS, GET THE FUCK OUT HERE.

I DON'T FUCKIN' CARE! I NEED TO SPEAK TO HIM NOW.
DAD! WHERE ARE W GOING?
GEORGE, I'M ON THE PHONE! JUS KEEP YOUR MOUTH SHU AND STAY I THE CAR.
WHAT THE FUCK, JIMMY?
THINGS'VE GONE TO SHIT HERE, MAN. I NEED YOUR HELP.
WHAT'RE YOU TALKIN' ABOUT?
THE GIRLS. THEY KILLED JOHNNY AND ROB, AND THAT TRAITOR FUCK TOMMY'S WORKING FOR 'EM.
I NEED SOMEWHERE TO HIDE OUT 'TIL IT BLOWS OVER.
AN' WHY THE FUCK SHOULD I HELP YOU?
WE HAVE A FUCKIN' DEAL, GARGANO.
FUCK THE DEAL, YOU WORTHLESS PIECE OF SHIT. WHAT USE ARE YOU TO ME NOW?
YOU STILL NEED ME TO GET AT TONY FOR YOU, YOU BACKSTABBIN' FUCK.
TONY'S DEAD, JIMMY, SO NO, I DON'T STILL FUCKIN' NEED YOU.
NOW I SUGGEST YOU GET THE FUCK OUTTA TOWN BEFORE--
DAD?

WHEN ARE WE GOING HOME? I'M TIRED.
I TOLD YOU TO STAY IN THE FUCKIN' CAR, GEORGE.
JIMMY...HAVE YOU GOT YOUR KIDS WITH YOU?
YEAH. WHAT WAS I GONNA DO, LET THAT BITCH KEEP 'EM?
FOR FUCK'S SAKE...
SONNY! GET IN HERE!
YEAH, OKAY, JIMMY. I'LL MEET YOU AT MATRANGA'S. BRING THE KIDS, AND I'LL HELP YOU OUT.
BRING THE CAR 'ROUND AND GET A COUPLA' THE GUYS UP HERE. WE'RE GONNA HAVE A BUSY FUCKIN' NIGHT.

I DON'T KNOW WHERE HE IS!
WE KNOW HE'S BEEN FUCKIN' HIDIN' HERE, JACK.
YOU THINK I WOULDN'T FUCKIN' FIND OUT?
WHAT WAS I GONNA DO, KATH? HE'S MY UNCLE, I COULDN'T SAY NO TO HIM.
BUT YOU GOTTA BELIEVE ME, I AIN'T SEEN HIM IN DAYS--
CRACK

AH, FUCK!
I DON'T KNOW WHERE HE FUCKING IS, OKAY?!
YOU LYING PIECE OF SHIT!
KATH, GO OUTSIDE.
OKAY...
WAIT! I DON'T KNOW ANYTHIN'!
PLEASE, KATH, YOU CAN'T DO THIS!
WE'RE FAMILY!

GYAAAAHH!
HOW'D IT HAPPEN? JIMMY AND THE KIDS?
HEATHER WAS BABYSITTIN'. HE BROKE IN THE HOUSE, SMACKED HER AROUND, AND DRAGGED THEM OUT TO HIS CAR--
SHE OKAY?
YEAH. SHOOK UP... BUT SHE'S OKAY.
SHE AIN'T GONNA TALK TO THE COPS, IS SHE?
DON'T START WITH THIS FUCKIN' BULLSHIT, RAVEN. NOT NOW.
I'M JUST SAYIN', PEOPLE DO STUPID SHIT WHEN THEY'RE SCARED, AND SHE KNOWS A LOT ABOUT WHAT WE DO.
JUST SHUT THE FUCK UP!
AAAAIIIHHHG!
BAM BAM
I'M SORRY, KATH... THIS AIN'T THE TIME TO TALK ABOUT IT.
I'M TIRED, RAVEN.
I KNOW, IT'S BEEN A LONG NIGHT.
I DON'T MEAN TONIGHT, I--
HE DIDN'T KNOW NOTHIN'.
WE SHOULD PROBABLY HEAD BACK TO CASEY'S AND SEE IF ANYONE'S CALLED.

CASEY'S
OWEN, TAKE HEATHER BACK INSIDE.

KATH. I'M SO SORRY FOR ALL YOU'VE BEEN THROUGH. A MOTHER SHOULD NEVER HAVE HER CHILDREN TAKEN FROM HER.
IT'S UNFORGIVABLE.
SONNY, CAN YOU?
TAKE THIS AS A GESTURE OF GOODWILL FROM ME TO YOU. FOR ANY PAST WRONGDOING ON MY PART.
WHAT THE FUCK'RE YOU TALKIN' ABOUT--?
HHMFMMFF!!

WHERE ARE MY KIDS?
THEY'RE WITH MY WIFE. SHE LOVES THE LITTLE BAMBINOS.
OKAY. GET THIS FUCK INSIDE. DON'T FUCKIN' TOUCH HIM 'TIL I GET BACK--
NO. I'LL TAKE RAVEN TO COLLECT THE CHILDREN.
WE NEED TO TALK BUSINESS, DON' WE, RAVEN?
YEAH, I GUESS WE DO...
?
FINE. YOU GO, RAVEN.
JUST BRING MY KIDS BACK TO ME.

McKINNON'S
OUR FUCKIN' KIDS!
YOU GET OUR FUCKIN' KIDS INVOLVED IN THIS?!

SMAK
KRAK

HEY, HOW YOU DOIN'?
OKAY, I GUESS... WHERE'S OWEN?
HE WENT HOME.
WHAT A FUCKIN' NIGHT.
HOW'S YOUR **FACE?**
IT'S FINE...
I COULDN'T STOP HIM, KATH. I **TRIED,** BUT--
IT AIN'T YOUR FAULT. THERE'S **NOTHIN'** YOU COULDA' DONE.
IT'S **MY** FUCKIN' FAULT. SOMETHING LIKE THIS WAS **ALWAYS** GONNA HAPPEN.

BUT MY FUCKIN' KIDS. I JUST...
IT'S ALL JUST TOO FUCKIN' MUCH, ALL THIS SHIT. I NEED TO GET OUT.
AH, FUCK, KATH. IT'LL BE OKAY. I'M HERE FOR YOU AND I AIN'T GOIN' NOWHERE.
CASEY

MONTHS AFTER.

71-0471

CBGB
OMFUG
315
315

I DON'T GIVE A FUCK, RAVEN.
WE'RE NOT DOIN' IT.
WHY NOT?
WHY?!?
'CAUSE HE DOESN'T DESERVE IT!
WHEN THE FUCK DID THAT MATTER, ANGIE?
I NEVER KILLED ANYONE WHO DIDN'T HAVE IT COMIN'.
WELL, LUCKY YOU.

LOOK, GARGANO WANTS HIM GONE, SO--
SO TELL GARGANO TO GET OFF HIS FAT ASS AND DO IT HIM-SELF.
YOU SURE YOU WANNA GO DOWN THIS ROAD, TOMMY?
FUCK HIM, AND FUCK YOU. WE'RE NOT GONNA KILL THIS GUY JUST 'CAUSE THAT PRICK TELLS US TO--
D'YOU SEE GARGANO HERE?! DO YOU?
IT'S ME RIGHT HERE TELLIN' YOU TO FUCKIN' DO THIS.
AND SINCE WHEN DO WE WORK FOR YOU?

I'M THE REASON YOU'RE NOT IN PRISON OR DEAD RIGHT NOW.
IF YOU WANNA KEEP IT THAT WAY, MAYBE YOU SHOULD FUCKIN' REMEMBER THAT.
YOU DON'T WANNA DO IT THIS WAY.
WHAT OTHER WAY IS THERE, TOMMY?

FOR CHRIST'S SAKE, CAN'T YOU SAY SOMETHIN' TO HER?
WE DON'T TALK MUCH THESE DAYS.
THERE'S SOMETHIN' YOU'VE GOTTA KNOW, KATH.
ME AND TOMMY, WE'VE BEEN TALKIN' AND...WE'RE LEAVIN' TOWN TOMORROW.
WHAT'RE YOU TALKIN' ABOUT?
WE CAN'T PUT UP WITH THIS CRAP NO MORE.
I KNOW SHE'S BEEN A PRICK LATELY, BUT SHE'S STILL--
YOU'VE BEEN SO WRAPPED UP WITH THIS SHIT WITH HEATHER GOIN' MISSIN' THAT YOU AIN'T BEEN PAYIN' ATTENTION.
DON'T YOU THINK SOMETHIN' STINKS ABOUT EVERY-THIN' THAT'S BEEN GOIN' ON?
TONY GETTIN' WHACKED THE SAME NIGHT SHE KILLED JOHNNY? FRANKY MYSTERIOUSLY DYIN' JUST BEFORE HE COULD TALK TO THE COPS?
WHAT YOU SAYIN'? RAVEN KILLED TONY AND FRANKY?
WE'RE SAYIN' THAT SHE AIN'T TELLIN' US EVERYTHIN' ABOUT HOW SHE SUDDENLY BECAME OUR FUCKIN' BOSS.

SHE DIDN'T KILL FRANKY. SHE DIDN'T HAVE THE REACH BACK THEN.
BUT THE NIGHT'VE THE BLACKOUT. SHE SAID SOMETHIN' TO ME, AND I DIDN'T THINK NOTHIN' OF IT THEN, BUT...YEAH, I THINK SHE KILLED TONY.
BUT FRANKY... WHO DO WE KNOW WHO DOES HAVE THAT KINDA REACH?
GARGANO...
MAYBE...MAYBE WE'RE JUST BEIN' PARANOID. BUT SOMETHIN'S FUCKIN' GOIN' ON HERE.
AND WE DON'T WANT NO PART IN ALL THIS BACKSTABBIN' BULLSHIT.
GEORGE AND JAMES JUNIOR ARE STILL STAYIN' WITH FAMILY, RIGHT?
YEAH...
YOU SHOULD COME WITH US, KATH. YOU DON'T NEED TO BE SUCKED INTO THIS MESS.
FUCK. EVEN IF IT'S ALL TRUE, I CAN'T GO 'TIL I'VE FOUND HEATHER.
C'MON, KATH, SHE PROBABLY SKIPPED TOWN 'CAUSE OF ALL THE SHIT WITH JIMMY.
SHE WOULDN'T'VE LEFT WITHOUT TELLIN' ME...
OKAY, IF YOU THINK YOU CAN, YOU GO FIND HER.
BUT LOOK AFTER YOURSELF, KATH--

"--AND WATCH YOUR BACK."

I LIKE THE NEW PLACE...
THANKS...

SO... WHAT'S UP?
I KNOW I AIN'T BEEN MUCH HELP LATELY. I JUST...YOU KNOW, AFTER EVERYTHIN' WITH JIMMY AND THE KIDS, I KINDA LOST HEART IN ALL THIS.

BUT YOU KNOW YOU CAN ALWAYS TALK TO ME, RIGHT?
IT DON'T MATTER WHAT HAPPENED, WHAT WE'VE DONE, WE'RE STILL SISTERS, AND I WANNA BE THERE FOR YOU.

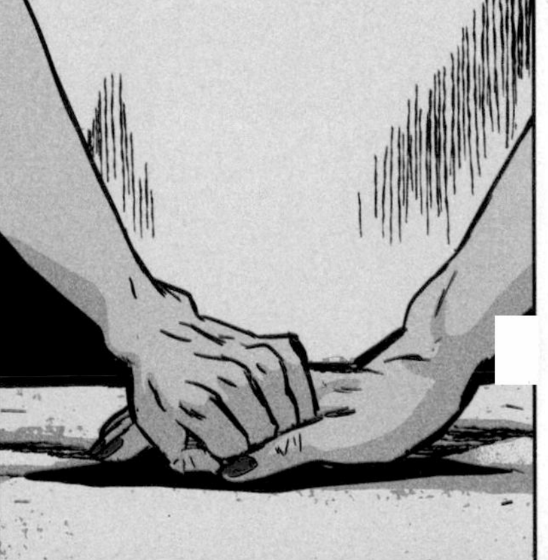

YOU KILLED TONY, DIDN'T YOU...?
FUCK...
HOW D'YOU KNOW?
JESUS, RAVEN. WHY'D YOU DO IT?
IT'S LIKE TOMMY SAID BACK BEFORE OUR MEET WITH GARGANO, THESE ITALIANS...
THEY ALL TALK ABOUT HONOR AND THEIR CODE, BUT THEY'RE ALWAYS FUCKIN' EACH OTHER OVER.
FUCK...I DID IT TO PROTECT THE CREW, KATH. TO PROTECT US.
WHY THE FUCK DIDN'T YOU TELL ME?!
YOU EVER KILLED ANYONE? SOMEONE YOU REALLY CARED ABOUT?
IT AIN'T SOMETHIN' YOU EVER WANNA TALK ABOUT.

WHY DIDN'T YOU KILL FRANKY?
WHAT?
YOU SAID YOU WANTED TO TALK, SO LET'S TALK.
BACK IN THAT ALLEYWAY, WHEN WE FOUND OUT WHO HE WAS. WHY DIDN'T YOU KILL HIM?
JUST FUCKIN' GET HIM OUTTA THE WAY, THERE AND THEN.
I DUNNO. WE WEREN'T REALLY THINKIN', WERE WE? IT ALL JUST HAPPENED.
FUCK... MAYBE I JUST COULDN'T BRING MYSELF TO DO IT.
I COULDN'T EVEN FINISH OFF JIMMY WHEN IT CAME TO IT... ANGIE HAD TO FUCKIN' DO IT.
AND THERE WAS ME, THINKIN' I WAS SOME BIG-SHOT GANGSTER.
YOU KNOW WHAT GARGANO SAID TO ME? HE SAID YOU DIDN'T HAVE THE HEART FOR THIS.
REALLY? I GUESS THAT GUINEA FUCK'S SMARTER THAN HE LOOKS.
HOW DID WE END UP HERE?
WHO THE FUCK KNOWS...

OKAY, NO MORE SECRETS.
I...I KILLED HEATHER.
WHAT?
SHE WAS A FUCKIN' JUNKIE, KATH. YOU CAN'T TRUST A JUNKIE.
SHE KNEW TOO MUCH ABOUT US...IF SHE'D SPOKEN TO THE COPS, OR ANOTHER CREW...
I DID IT TO PROTECT US, KATH. SAME AS WITH TONY--

IT'S NOT THE FUCKIN' SAME! SHE DIDN'T DESERVE THAT!
SHE WOULDA' GOT US ALL FUCKIN' KILLED, KATH!
MMMPPH GET THE FUCK OFFA ME!

SMAK
YOU HEARTLESS FUCKIN' BITCH!
SOK
IF ONLY DAD WAS ALIVE TODAY, HE WOULDA' BEEN FUCKIN' PROUD TO SEE THE SCUMBAG YOU TURNED INTO!
LIKE FATHER, LIKE FUCKIN' DAUGHTER--
KLOK

...I'M NOT THE FUCKIN' SAME...

KATH?

"KATH!"
ONE YEAR LATER.
WHY THE FUCK DID I NEED TO BE HERE?
HE'S THE GUY WHO'S BEEN HITTIN' OUR TRUCKS--
YOU KNOW IT WAS HIM? JUST FUCKIN' KILL 'IM.
DON'T GET SENTIMENTAL WITH THESE PRICKS, AND DON'T FUCKIN' WASTE MY TIME.
I'M SORRY, BOSS--
I COULD GIVE A FUCK IF YOU'RE SORRY, JUST DON'T DO IT AGAIN.

Vincenzo's
CASEY'S PUB
Vincenzo's

ANGIE, LISTEN, WE CAN FUCKIN' TALK ABOUT THIS. YOU DON'T KNOW WHAT HAPPENED. I...
YOU KNOW WHAT? FUCK YOU! I DID WHAT NEEDED TO BE DONE.
THEY'RE GONNA REMEMBER MY NAME AFTER I DIE. NOT MY DAD'S, NOT JOHNNY'S OR JIMMY'S. MINE.
I MADE MY MARK ON THE FUCKIN' WORLD. I--
OKAY. JUST FUCKIN'--
BAM

TO THE
END